Curious Christopher

Robin Campbell

Published by

Impression Publishing

www.impressionpublishing.net

First Edition published 2013

© Robin Campbell 2013

Printed and bound in Great Britain by

www.printandpublish.co.uk

A catalogue record for this book

is available from The British Library

ISBN 978-1-908374-83-7

Contents

Chapter 1 My Name's Christopher – I Think

I knew it was going to be tough getting to be one year old. I knew it right from the start. There was I, minding my own business, and all tucked up inside my mum. Of course, I had to move around a bit and have a stretch from time-to-time. When I had a stretch I could hear my mum telling my dad that I was on the move.

'Here, feel this; I think it's a foot.'

What a strange thing to say. Of course it was my foot. Sometimes it seemed to get caught up and I needed to stretch my leg out so that I didn't get pins and needles. But apart from that I was very comfortable. I was getting all the food that I needed through my belly button and it seemed that I could eat whenever I wanted. Yes, it was very comfortable waiting to get born.

Then all of a sudden it happened. Before I had a chance to have any say in the matter I was on my way out into the big wide world. All I had done was to stretch a bit more frequently as it was getting very cramped. That seemed to start a great commotion. Down the road we went in an ambulance, blue lights flashing and sirens sounding.

I really enjoyed that trip. I had been on lots of journeys in a car, but that was nothing compared to travelling in an ambulance. I'd like to have a ride in an ambulance again one day but sitting up so that I can see what's was going on. This time the journey didn't last long and once we got into hospital it was less pleasant. I was wheeled into the hospital – well my mum was, and of course I was with her. Then once we were in the delivery room I pushed and was pulled out into the world. What a journey that was! It was nowhere near as good as travelling in the ambulance. And it took hours and hours. I'm not doing that again. Now that I'm out I'm staying out.

I was curious to see the world, but it was horrible when I first got out. I was covered in yuk. So, what did the doctor and nurses do first? Held me by my ankles so that I was upside down, and then they gave me a really hard pat on my back. It was enough to make me spit out a load of yukky stuff from my mouth. Then I gave the loudest yell I possibly could, just to tell everyone what I thought about my arrival and the way I was being treated. That seemed to work because a nurse took me next door into a smaller room and gave me a good clean up all over, then looked at my toes and fingers, and finally weighed me.

'Who's a big boy?'

Well, it's me, of course. What a stupid question to ask. There was only me and the nurse in the room. Who else was there but me that could be the big boy? Still, I quite liked the soft muslin blanket she wrapped me in. It seemed to curl all round me and made me feel secure and comfortable, just like I had been before I was born. Then we left the smaller room.

One of the other nurses must have helped my mum to get tidy because by the time we got back into the larger room she was propped up in the bed. Then as soon as she saw me she held out her arms out for me.

'Here's your son,' said the nurse as she handed me over. 'And he weighs eight and a half pounds.'

Perhaps it was the extra half pound that made the nurse think I was a big boy. Eight and half pounds, yes – that sounded good. And it must have been good because everyone smiled.

'Hello, Christopher,' said my mum.

I don't know if she expected me to reply but any way I just looked at her and that was enough to get her crying so perhaps it was best not to try and talk. I'll leave that for later, I thought.

My dad arrived next. I recognised him from the sound of his footsteps. He was taller than I had expected. I thought he would come over and see me first. But, can you believe it? Before he even looked at me he gave my mum a kiss.

'Hey dad, don't you recognise me?' I thought to myself.

'Hey, Christo, how you going?'

Christo! Whatever happened to the 'pher'. Christopher didn't last long as my name did it? I'd only been around for a matter of minutes and already I had been called big boy, son, Christopher and Christo. Whatever next I wondered? Then I saw my Grandma and Granddad for the first time.

They're really my mum's mum and dad, but that means I get to call them grandma and granddad.

'So, it is a little man, is it?' said granddad.

So that's another name then. This time, instead of being a big boy I'm now a little man; oh well.

'Christopher,' said my mum by way of a reply.

'Chris, I like that,' said granddad.

Here we go again, I thought, that is another two letters I've lost. Is anyone going to drop a few more and call me 'Chr', or if they drop those letters instead I'll be left with just 'is'. Still, at the moment the choice seems to be big boy, son, Christopher, Christo, little man or Chris. I think I would like to stay as Christopher for the moment. That's what my mum called me and she should know because she looked after me for the nine months before I was even born.

Chapter 2 Drinking Milk

Mum had decided long ago that I was going to be bottle-fed. She and dad had discussed it over and over again.

'If he's on bottle milk you'll be able to feed him in the evenings, and at weekends,' she told my dad.

I think that was really the important reason for my mum deciding I was going to be bottle-fed. Mum wanted to have a break from looking after me all day and all night. She was right. Sometimes it seemed as though I got hungrier during the night than I did during the day. After all in the day there is a lot I'm curious to see and understand. So I'm very busy in the daytime. Even though at first I could only lie on my back and look around – and that was blurred to start with – still that was better than being in my cot at night. I couldn't see a thing.

And it was at night that I would feel really hungry. So what I would do was to cry out. Then cry a bit louder. Then, if no milk came, I would just cry and scream as loud as I could. It didn't take long then for mum or dad to come into my room with a lovely bottle of milk. I could see it was going to be a bit of a job to train my parents to bring me some milk whenever I felt like it. But in the end it didn't take as long as I thought it might. Within a week I had them at my beck and call – I should really say my cry and scream.

The strange thing was that once I got them to do exactly what I wanted them to do I started to get more tired at night. It was a hard job to wake up and scream for milk. Then one night they put me to bed and the next thing I knew it was morning time. Both mum and dad were by my cot 'cooing' and 'ooing' to wake me up. I'd slept all through the night without having a drink. You'd think I had won the lottery for them. They made such a fuss of me for going all through the night without having a drink. But the more they went on cooing, the more I realised I was really thirsty. I knew it would have to come. If they couldn't work out that I needed some milk badly then I would have to let them know. So I took a deep breath and then screamed at the top of my voice. Boy, did that make them jump.

'I think he needs some milk,' said my mum.

'Good guess,' I thought.

I let out another scream, just to let her know that she had got it right.

But drinking milk is not as easy as it might look. For a start there are different sizes of holes to suck the milk through. I like the middle size best. Then you can just suck gently and get a nice steady flow of milk going down your throat. It's super. Mum tried me with the large hole at first. I heard her tell my dad all about it.

'This will be best, he'll be able to get the milk easily and be done in next to no time.'

'Good, then perhaps he won't take ages at night.'

Hm! Here was me thinking that my dad liked to come and feed me in the middle of the night, when all the time he was trying to get it done as soon as possible. Still the large hole was useless. One suck and I was choking with all the milk that came out. That made me gulp down some air so the next thing was I had the biggest burp I've ever heard.

'Take it steady, Christopher.'

Honestly at times I wonder about my parents. What did they think I was trying to do? Anyway I tried again and still far too much came out. At least this time it just dribbled all down my chin and on to my top. That was another yuk. It is really horrible having a top on that's covered in milk. It's cold, sticky and smelly and I really don't like it.

So, then they tried me with the smallest hole for drinking milk. That was hopeless. I had to suck so hard to get the tiniest bit of milk that it made my cheeks sore. Then by the time I had finished the bottle – and that was ages after I started – I was hungry again. It was really hard work to get a drink of milk.

Fortunately, in the end my parents came to their senses. They gave me a bottle with the middle size hole. And that was just right. It was like the story about Goldie someone or other and the three bears. Then it was the porridge that was too hot, too cold and just right. Now my drink was just right and I could enjoy my milk again.

Chapter 3 Time For Bed

I always have a drink of milk just before I go to bed. But that is only part of the routine. I know when I am going to bed because it's bath, book, milk and then bed. It's a set routine that my parents got into within a few weeks of me being born. They're weird my parents. They seem to think that I don't know what is happening when they ask me.

'Do you want to have a bath?'

It really means, it's nearly time for you to go to bed. But I don't like to create a scene, and I don't cry, because then they think I'm too tired to have a bath and I miss out on one of my favourite times of the day.

Bath time is great. At first I wasn't too sure. So many things went wrong to start with. It took me a while to get used to the water. The temperature of the water, splashing too hard, the water in my face, slipping over and playing with toys; there's lots to learn.

My parents have to get the temperature just right or it's not so good. It's a bit like those three bears again, I don't like it too hot and I really, really don't like it too cold. It's best when it is just right. Then as soon as I was able to sit on my own – and that took a while – I started to splash. It's good fun.

I like to catch my parents when they're not paying attention. That's when I make the biggest splash possible. To make the big, big splash I have my hands flat and bring them down really hard on to the water. At first I thought I would get my best splash with my hand like a fist but no, it's a flat hand that's best. It's great. The splash goes everywhere and I soak my mum or dad. I don't do that straight away, because sometimes they get cross if I make them too wet and that's the bath finished before I really get started. So I leave the big splashes for later in the bath time.

Of course, at first I got frightened when I splashed too hard. The water shot up into my face. Some went up my nose and I couldn't see for a while because of the water in my eyes. But I soon learnt to splash a little way away from my body. That way the water goes in mum's and dad's faces and not mine. It's best to smile sweetly when I splash them, then they think it was an accident. But I know what I'm doing because I'm a really good splasher. When I am bit older I will have to be careful not to stand up when I'm splashing 'cos it's really easy to slip over and that gives me a bit of a fright.

Sometimes I don't do much splashing because I spend most of the time playing with my toys. One of my favourites is duck. Of course, it's not a real duck. They're at the pond that we sometimes walk to; well mum walks and I ride in my buggy. No, this is one of those yellow plastic ducks. They're good fun. You can fill them up if you hold it under the water and then they're great for squirting. I've got plastic fish that I can do that with as well. But duck is my favourite. I think it's because it was one of my first words when I had had my first birthday.

'Dk.'

It got mum and dad excited when I said duck for the first time. Now, whenever I'm in the bath mum or dad go on and on about it.

'Say, 'duck', it's 'duck,' isn't it.'

Sometimes I just ignore them so they keep on repeating again and again.

'Say, 'duck', it's 'duck,' isn't it.'

But then I usually say, 'Dk,' just to keep them happy.

Then it's out of the bath into the big fluffy towel. I like that because it's nice and warm and comfortable. Once I'm dry it's into my clean nappy and pyjamas and ready for a book, then milk and bed.

I've got some great books. There's that big purple bear, the cat with a red and white hat, and books with dogs and cats and lots of other animals. I'm best with the hardback books. Because although I'm very careful with my lovely books some of the paper books don't seem to be very strong. You only have to turn over a page and the page can easily tear away from the rest of the book. Really, I am best with the hardback books. And I don't mind who reads the book to me. Sometimes it's mum and sometimes, if he's home on time, it will be dad. Even grandma and granddad read to me when they are here on a visit. I just like the books, so I don't mind who does the reading just as long as they give me time to look at the pictures on each page.

After looking at a book or two, or even three or four of them, it's on to a bottle of milk. I don't know why it is, but the bottle of milk last thing at night seems to be really special. I just lie back in mum or dad's arms, and gently suck out the milk. I do it slowly and with each suck it just seems to make me go all cosy, dreamy and sleepy. Sometimes I fall asleep right there. At other times I get taken up to bed, put into my cot and I'm off before you can say, 'Jack Ro...bin...'

Chapter 4 My Toys

You wouldn't believe how many toys I've got. It all started when I was born. Everyone who came to see me brought me a toy. And every one was a fluffy animal. I mean the toys were all fluffy animals, not everyone who came to see me. Mum and dad, grandma and granddad, aunts and uncles, friends and partners – you name them and I'll tell you which fluffy animal they gave me. I've got bears and bears and bears. And I've got monkeys, some orang-u-tangs, and some chimpanzees and there is one gorilla that looks a bit fierce but is always gentle with me. I've even got a sheep, a lion and one that I think is a crocodile. My cot and room are full of fluffy animals and the daft thing is that when I first got them all I couldn't hold any of them – it was just too difficult. And I couldn't really see them very well, either.

Can you imagine how difficult it is to hold a fluffy animal, especially when you are only a few days old?

'Do you want to play with your orang-u-tang?' mum would ask me.

Well, of course I would, but for a start I couldn't really get my hands to come together in order to hold one. It's really hard to control both hands at the same time.

'Do you want to play with your orang-u-tang?'

Part of the trouble was that I couldn't quite see exactly where the animal was. So when I did move my arms around I usually seemed to be miles away from the toy. At other times I was too close and I just knocked it over.

'Do you want to play with your orang-u-tang?'

It took me quite a few months before I could see exactly where the animal was. Then I had to try to get my hands together to grab it. That wasn't easy. I could see my hands and eventually I got to know that they were at the end of each arm. But my arms wouldn't always do what I wanted them to do. They just seemed to wave about all over the place. None of those difficulties really mattered however. My mum just kept on asking.

'Do you want to play with your orang-u-tang?'

Still, as I got older I was able to get hold of one of my animals at a time and to cuddle it. Fluffy animals are lovely to cuddle, aren't they?

My favourite fluffy animal was the orang-u-tang. Even when I couldn't quite get hold of it I could usually grab one of its long arms or legs and pull it towards me. It didn't take very long before I had dribbled over it, and spilt some milk over it as well. So after a few months it wasn't quite so fluffy and lots of the hairs were stuck together. But the good thing about it was that even when it was very dark in my bed I could still find my orang-u-tang because it had a very gentle smell of me. It was my favourite toy to cuddle. When no one was around, or everyone was too busy to bother about me it was nice to have my favourite animal so that I didn't feel alone.

After that the toys just kept on coming. I got cars and planes, trains and helicopters, lorries and tractors, diggers and dump trucks, footballs – big and small. They all looked great but to start with they were pretty useless as well. I mean, how was I supposed to play football? I couldn't do anything except lie on my back and wave my arms about. Rolling over, crawling, standing and walking were all impossible for me; they would take months of hard work to develop. Still it was nice of all those people to be so kind to me.

The funny thing is that although I had all of those toys as I got older I liked to play with the box that they came in best of all. After all, the toy could usually only be whatever it was. A helicopter is a helicopter. The box could be lots of different things. Boxes are great. Some I can get into and they can be a train, tractor, digger or dump truck. The box can be whatever I want it to be. Or the other way round it can be a house, castle, lighthouse or tower. If it's a strong box I could, when I was older, even stand on top of it and see what's around above my head. Of course, as soon as I stood on a box you can imagine what my mum said.

'Be careful up there, you might fall.'

But falling seemed to be one of those things I had to get used to.

'Hold on tight,' was another of my mum's favourites. But often there was nothing to hold on tight to. It was good to have my fluffy toys around though. Because I could hold on tight to them, I could use them as a cushion or a bed; later they were good for throwing around.

I like my toys, and the boxes they come in. They are great. And although I've got more than I need, I think I'll keep quiet about that. You never know, I might want some new ones as I get older.

Chapter 5 Hello Christopher

'Hello, Christopher.'

People do like to say that to me. Of course, I still do get some other greetings like, 'Hello, Christo,' and, 'Hello, Chris'. My name is constantly chopped about. I've got used to that now. I just get a lot of helloes. I hope that none of them expect me to reply. I really can't get my lips and mouth to produce words. I do try but it just comes out as a sort of a 'ga, ga, ga.' I'm sure mum wants me to reply,

'Oh, hello, Uncle Bill. How are you today?'

There is no way I'm going to manage that for ages. Still a broad smile works wonders.

'Oh, what a lovely smile he's got.'

Yes, well sometimes I'm just feeling full of wind from having drunk a big bottle of milk. So it's a kind of burp from being too full that looks like a smile. Still, as long as it keeps the adults happy.

Sometimes the adults don't use my name. Instead they say something like,

'Who's a big boy now?'

Now that is really weird. Because you might remember that the first words ever spoken to me were, 'Who's a big boy?'

It was the nurse who said that, straight after I was born. Well, not exactly straight after, because first the nurse had whacked me on my back. So that I spat out all that yuk.

Still, the thing is how can I be big boy now when my nurse thought I was a big boy as soon as I was born? These adults really need to get their act together. A bit of consistency would be good. Otherwise how am I going to learn things? Was I big then or is it only now that I am big.

Then just to confuse the issue even more I sometimes get.

'Who's getting to be big boy?'

So I was a big boy when I was born. Or I'm getting to be a big boy. Or I'm a big boy now. This growing up is a really tricky business. But I think I've got quite a bit of growing to do because all the adults are really big. They make me feel quite small and not really big at all.

Of course, all these greetings can get worse. Some adults hardly say a word to me. They just look at me then turn and say to mum or dad – and it is usually mum – because dad is probably still at work.

'Isn't he lovely?'

They need to realise that most boys don't like to be told that they look lovely. Now handsome that's a different matter.

But it gets worse after you hear the dreaded words 'Isn't he lovely'. Watch out. There is probably a big slobbering kiss coming your way. I hate it when they do that to me. Yuk. It's different when mum and dad kiss me goodnight. They are always soft and gentle. No, it's the big slobbering kiss from distant relations and strangers I can't stand. I really hate it when they leave my face all wet. Yuk, and double yuk.

So there are those who hardly say a word to me. Then there are those who are the exact opposite. They just jabber away as soon as they see me.

'Hello, hello, hello,' or sometimes just, 'lo, lo, lo.'

Some adults seem to think I won't be able to cope with full words so they just chop them in half and expect me to understand what they are talking about.

There are some adults who use such strange adult talk.

'Who's a lovely liddle, liddle boy.'

'Doh, doh, doh.'

'Is that your chinny-chinny-chin.'

What on earth are they saying? I even heard one of my uncles say to my aunt, 'Don't use such baby talk.' Baby talk! I wouldn't dream of talking such rubbish. That's if I could talk. But really 'strange adult talk' is what I call it. I really can't make it out at all. The adults chop words in half, or change some of the letters. No wonder it is such hard work for me to understand what they are saying.

But there is one 'Hello Christopher' that I really like lots and lots. That's when right towards the end of the day when I'm getting really tired my dad comes indoors and says, 'Hello Christopher.' I think mum managed to get dad to say Christopher instead of Christo. And I know when he's getting close because mum lets me know that dad will be here soon, because he's finished at work. I'm not sure what this work thing is. I'm curious to find out about that later.

But dad always says, 'Hello Christopher,' and gives me a great big hug. I think he likes seeing me and I know I like seeing him.

Chapter 6 I'm Eating Real Food At Last

One of the things that I noticed very early on was how everyone else was eating real food while I only had my bottle of milk. Although, can you believe it, sometimes I didn't even get that. Instead it was just a bottle of water. Water is okay, but really it is my milk that I like best of all. Especially after my bath, when I'm getting ready for bed. This real food thing looked very interesting. I didn't know if I would be able to do the chewing but I really would like to give it a try.

The first thing I was given was what mum called a rusk. It just looked like a piece of crust from some toast. But it was good and I liked to hold it myself although I couldn't always find my mouth. I know that seems strange, because I know where my mouth is, it's just sometimes I can't find it.

I've prodded the crust up my nose, poked it in my eye and jabbed my chin with it. As you can imagine, the more times I had a crust the better I became at putting it into my mouth. At first I just kind of sucked on it. Later, when I learned to move my jaw up and down, I was almost looking like mum and dad when they eat their food. I was beginning to learn to chew.

At about the same time I started to have some food out of a tiny jar. That was really yummy. And it had all sort of different tastes.

'Would you like some potato and corn?' asked my mum.

How was I supposed to know? I'd never had potato and corn but it was good. And it was all kind of mushy so it was okay to swallow. After a few days there were other jars with different kinds of food to be tried.

'Would you like a dessert?' said mum.

'Or shall we call it pudding?'

'Here we are, try this strawberry and cream.'

Now that was something else. Real yummy, yummy. It was sweet and easy to slide down my throat. This real food business was going to be good. Mind you, I didn't always get all of the food to slide down my throat. Somehow it seemed to escape from my mouth and slide down my chin. Good job I had a bib on or there would have been a real mess. And sometimes there was a mess all over my chin, down the bib and on to whatever clothes I was wearing. I got it everywhere.

Then there was the time when the phone went just as mum was giving me a jar of food. So off she went to the phone in the kitchen. She left the food on the tray of my high-chair. I was able to get hold of it and put my fingers into the jar to get some food. It almost worked really well.

But I wasn't as good at it as my mum. I couldn't always get my fingers from the jar to my mouth. So a lot went on to my chin, bib, clothes, tray and even the floor.

I know I didn't do very well because when mum came back she said, 'Oh, Christopher, what have you done?'

Can you believe the next thing she did was to burst out laughing?

'You're a right mess,' she said, then carried on laughing.

Of course, I did have other things to eat. Like when I was a little bit older mum said, 'Shall we try some fruit?'

What am I supposed to say? I didn't even know what fruit was. But once I found out it was lovely. First of all it was a small piece of banana which mum cut from the big fruit. Then she mashed it up and fed me from a spoon. That was good; I enjoyed that. But there were so many different kinds of fruit that I got to like. Mum peeled the skin off nectarines, apples and pears. Then cut little pieces off for me to have. That was lovely. I like fruit. Then I got to have a small piece of strawberry and that was even better than mushy strawberry from a jar.

But I noticed one night mum and dad had some ice-cream with their strawberries – I didn't get any of that. And the way that they ate it made me think it was probably really nice. I think I'm going to like ice-cream once I get to try it. And there are lots of different colours. So it's not just one ice-cream that I need to try; there are lots to be tried just as soon as I can get mum and dad to give me some. I am really curious to see which I will like best of all.

And then they had some crusts, well they looked like crusts but they called them biscuits. And they had chocolate on them. So they called them chocolate biscuits. But no way did I get to have one of them. Mum and dad seemed to try and hide them from me. That makes me think they are probably very tasty. Later I'll have to work out a way to ask for one or two of those. They seemed to be as good as the ice-cream. I think I'll get to like those as well once I get a chance to try them.

Chapter 7 Here Come My Teeth

I knew fairly early on that I would have to get some of those white things in my mouth. All the adults have them and most of the older children as well. They call them teeth. So that's what I needed to get. I thought they would be a great help when I try some of those chocolate biscuits that mum and dad hide from me.

Really I'd like to have teeth like my granddad. They're great. I have seen them when I've been lying on the floor in the bathroom waiting to have a clean nappy. Granddad just takes out his teeth, brushes them with his toothbrush, and then puts them back in his mouth. How cool is that? But most people can't do that; they just have to brush their teeth in their mouth. That looks a bit tricky but I think I'll be able to do it when I'm older.

'Ouch.'

What I didn't know was how painful getting each of my teeth was going to be.

'Ouch.'

They really hurt when they are trying to come through. Of course, they don't come straight away. I was seven months old before the first of my teeth came. It was at the front and at the bottom.

'Look he's got a tooth, bottom left,' explained my mum to anyone who wanted to know.

And it seemed that mum wanted to tell everyone about it. You'd think I'd won the lottery, whatever winning the lottery means. I've heard grandma say she'd like to win the lottery. So I think it must be something good.

What mum didn't mention to anyone was the agony of getting each tooth. She didn't seem to realise at first just how sore my gums felt. Sometime it was just an overall dull pain. But at other times it was really strong, sharp jabs.

'Ouch.'

Those chocolate biscuits better be worth it I thought, because this was agony. So, I had to tell my mum just how painful the sharp jabs were.

'Ouch.'

'Ya, Ya, Ya.'

I screamed as loud as I possibly could.

'What's the matter? Have you got a stomach ache?' she asked the first time I yelled.

Of course I haven't. It's not my stomach. It's my teeth. She didn't seem to understand.

'Do you need a clean nappy?' she asked.

Of course I don't, it's my teeth. She really didn't understand.

'Are you getting a tooth through?' she finally managed to ask.

Then she rubbed my gums with her finger. That was quite soothing. I just hoped she would be ready to do that at night as well as during the day.

My gums were sore most of the day. Luckily mum had taken me in my buggy to the chemist. And she bought a tiny bottle of something. Then, whenever my teeth were really sore she put some of the liquid from the bottle on to her finger and then rubbed that on to my gums. That really helped and it made it all a bit less painful. And it was quite tasty as well.

The trouble was that my gums and teeth were really much worse at night.

'Ouch, and double ouch.'

It seemed like each tooth wanted to push through my gums at night.

'Ouch, and double ouch.'

So I just had to yell at the top of my voice to get mum or dad to come and rub my gums.

'Ouch, and double ouch.'

And it was best if they put some of that medicine on their finger first. Then just gently rubbed over my gum where the tooth was trying to come through. That made it a bit better, but I don't think mum and dad realised just how sore my gums were. I even heard my dad say,

'I'll be glad when all his teeth are through.'

What about me, dad? Can you imagine how pleased I'm going to be when my all my teeth are through? I know it's going to be good. First of all, there will be no more agony;

and second, I really do think I'll be able to do well with eating real food, especially those chocolate biscuits.

Even when I got my four front teeth eating became really interesting. I had two teeth at the top and two at the bottom. That meant I was able to nibble at those crust things that mum gave me. It was much better that just sucking on them. I think my teeth are really good ones because they helped me to nibble away really well.

And mum and dad and the grandparents and everyone else I saw all said, 'You've got lovely teeth.'

So I think that my teeth are okay. It took a while for me to get all my teeth. And I didn't realise just how sore my gums would get when the back teeth were coming through. We all had some sleepless nights when that happened.

'Ouch, and double, double ouch.'

Chapter 8 I Hate Nappies

You might think I would like nappies. After all, they've got great pictures on them. You wouldn't believe all the different pictures that you can get on your nappies. I've had dinosaur nappies with lots of different pictures of those big huge animals. Not that I've seen any dinosaurs around where I live. But I have seen cats and dogs near our house and all sorts of different birds fly by when we are out and about.

Instead of dinosaurs you can just have pictures of cartoon characters on the nappies. They're good fun and I quite like them. Not that I know a lot of the characters but I have seen a few on the TV. Sometimes, when mum is really tired, she puts on the television so we can watch a cartoon. I think she only does it to have a rest.

And then there are nappies with other animals on. So I've had lion nappies and zebra ones. So there are lots of interesting nappies. I get to know the names of the nappy creatures because my mum says things like.

'Do want your zebra nappy on?'

So that's how I've got to know about them. And I know when I wear them the nappies stop all my clothes from getting in a mess. So you would think I might like nappies. But no way do I like nappies.

The trouble is that it is really hard to move with a big nappy on. Can you imagine how you would feel if you had a great big wodge of cotton and cloth wrapped round your middle. You really can't move well at all. I mean once I had got over my birth, which was really hard work, I wanted to move. But it was a real struggle to roll over or sit up or do anything except just lie there on the floor, or the chair, or the sofa. Moving was almost impossible with a ton weight round my 'tum'. Just about the only thing I could do was to move my legs up and down. Then, if it was not soft under my feet like lying on a carpet, a cushion or a sofa; it was really sore when I banged my feet on the ground. The trouble was I couldn't easily see over my nappy to see where the floor was and my feet hit the ground too hard.

So nappies were not my favourite piece of clothing. And it just got worse. The trouble is that when a nappy gets wet it just gets heavier and heavier. I don't think mum always knows just how wet and heavy my nappy sometimes get. Of course, it got worse when I learnt to stand up. I'll tell you about standing up later. But when I was standing up with a wet nappy on, it felt even heavier. And the heavy wet nappy just dragged my trousers lower and lower until it became almost impossible to stand. And walking with a heavy wet nappy was a no go area, at least at first it was.

But it's not just a heavy wet nappy that is a nuisance. At some time every day I do a poo in my nappy and that is really horrible. The trouble is I don't know that it's coming and then all of a sudden there it is and it's horrible. Whenever it happens I make as much noise as possible so that mum knows I need a new nappy. The trouble is she doesn't always realise straight away what is happening. So I have to wait and wait for her to get the message and all of that time I've got a poo nappy on.

'Yuk.'

Still, eventually she gets the message, and then usually says something stupid like, 'Would you like a clean nappy?'

I mean what a question. Of course I want a clean nappy and I want it just as quickly as possible. Still, once mum knows that I need a new nappy she's very good. She carries me up to the bathroom, puts me on the floor and takes off the dirty nappy and wipes me nice and clean. That's great because as well as getting rid of the horrible dirty nappy I also get the chance to have a good kick with my legs. It's brilliant without a nappy on. I can move so much better. No wonder I hate nappies.

So I'll be really glad to get rid of nappies when I'm a bit older. But I did find out that nappies can be really good at times. It took me quite a while to work how to stand up. Then I kept falling over. But it didn't hurt because the big bulky nappy gave me a lovely soft landing. It was great. So perhaps I'll try to keep in nappies until I get really steady on my feet. Then once I've stopped falling over I'll get rid of my nappies.

'Hooray!'

Chapter 9 I'm Starting To Crawl

I think the first time I rolled over it was a bit of an accident. I was lying on my back looking at the ceiling. Usually I had my mobile frame above my head to play with. The mobiles are good fun. There are lots of different soft animals hanging from the mobile. Sometimes I try to touch one of the animals, but it is not as easy as you might think. I don't always manage to get my hand in the right place to touch an animal.

Anyway on this morning I was just lying on the floor. I think I kept swinging my right arm over towards my left side. Then I swung it so hard that I pulled my whole body over and, 'plonk,' I was on my tummy. So now all I could see was the floor. I tried to lift my head up and I managed to do that for a moment. But it's quite hard on the neck muscles so I quickly had to put my face on the floor again.

Then mum saw me.

'How did you do that?' mum asked.

I would have told her all about it but the trouble is my talking is about the same as my rolling. I've still got lots to learn.

'There we are,' said mum as she put me on my back again.

Of course, now that I had been on my stomach once I wanted to try and do it again. You'd be surprised just how hard it was to do it again. Eventually I gave a really big swing and I was over again. I had to wait until my mum noticed before I could get on to my back once more, but at least I think I had sorted out moving from my back to my front. Once I got it going I could do it whenever I wanted.

Then I managed one morning to get from my stomach on to my back without having to wait for my mum to help me.

So now I could lie on my back, roll on to my stomach and then roll again on to my back. It was great. The funny thing was that if I kept on rolling I finished off in a whole lot of different places. I reached the bottom of the stairs – I think it will be a while before I can get up them. I rolled all the way to the table and finished up underneath the table and in between two of the chairs. I really couldn't move anywhere then until mum rescued me. So I could roll all around the room. The trouble was I couldn't decide where I wanted to go. I just had to wait to see where I landed up. No, if I wanted to go where I wanted to go I would have to learn to crawl.

I knew about crawling. Mum, and sometimes dad, used to take me to the library. In the children's section there are an incredible number of books to look at. But there are also chairs for the adults and a lot of space for the children. And I have watched as lots of children crawl around the floor. It's funny really, because there seems to be so many different styles of crawling. Some children crawl on their hands and knees, some do it on their hands and feet which looked a bit harder. I've even seen a few who seemed to crawl really close to the floor. My dad called it the commando crawl. And I saw one boy – I think it was boy because he was wearing a blue top – he used a brick under each hand and used those like a slide to whizz across the floor. The trouble was that it was no good once he got to a carpet. Then the sliders wouldn't work.

I decided the best way of doing it was going to be using the simple hands and knees crawl. The trouble was it was not as easy to do as you might think. For a start I had to find a way to push my body up so that my arms could hold me up. It was not easy. You really need strong arms for crawling. And it's a bit hard on the knees to be crawling around on the floor. But I did it. I could crawl. Now I could start to explore the house where I lived. Mind you, by the end of my first day of crawling I was really tired. My arms ached and my knees were sore. I slept like a log that night. I was so tired I didn't even know if my gums were sore or not. I just slept.

'If he's going to sleep like that he can crawl all day,' I heard my dad say. Mum was not so sure.

'The trouble is I'll never know where he is,' said my worried mum.

She was right. I could crawl and I would be able to go anywhere. Although probably not climbing up the stairs. That looked far too tricky. But I could crawl around the big room, into the hall and along to the kitchen. It was great fun. I didn't have to wait to be picked up. I could just go anywhere.

Chapter 10 I Can Stand And Walk, But I Do Wobble

I knew it would happen. As soon as I began to crawl around the house I began to wonder about standing up. It's what most people that I see do. The trouble is, it looks along way up and I'm not sure my legs are strong enough to support me. But first of all I have to work out how I'm going to get up into a standing position. It's not going to be easy.

I can roll quite easily now. And I can roll either to the left or to the right. So, I'm a good roller. And I can sit up on the floor. Although I do prefer it when mum or dad put one, two or three really big cushions behind me and on each side. That way it's harder to topple over because I do wobble. It also stops me from bumping my head. But standing is different. Still, if so many people can do it why not me too?

What I did to start with was to crawl over to the big soft sofa. The seat on the sofa is not very high. Then I grabbed hold of the seat part of the sofa and started to pull myself up. Not easy. I had to pull hard with my arms, push with my legs and keep a hold on the sofa to stop me from falling. It was really hard work and of course I was no sooner up there then I fell straight back down. That's when I found out that nappies are good for when I fall over. They really do give me good protection when I fall. And the first time I stood up no one saw me do it. Can you imagine it! A great personal achievement and no one was there to witness it.

Luckily the second time I stood up mum was just coming in from the kitchen. So she saw me do it.

'Who's a clever boy?' she asked. I'm not sure if I was supposed to say,

'It was me, mum, I did it.'

But I can't do that amount of talking, so I just smiled and did one of those gurgles that she seems to like so much.

Of course, I had to do the standing up again when my dad got home. I was really tired by the time I did it for dad. I thought I might not be able to do another single stand up, but I did it.

'Who's a clever boy?' he asked.

You would think dad might have come up with something original, but no, the same old thing about me being a clever boy.

As it was nearly bath time I noticed my wet nappy. It was really heavy when I was standing up. I think if I had stayed standing for too long the nappy would have reached my ankles. Luckily again dad scooped me up and took me upstairs for my bath.

The next day was really tiring. I spent a lot of the day pulling myself up next to the sofa and then falling down again. I thought about trying to take a step or two so that I would be walking. But it was really quite frightening. Beginning to walk was going to be hard. I think adults have forgotten how difficult it is. You have to take one foot off the ground and move it forward to a new position before doing the same with the other foot. It means that for a fraction of a second you've only got one foot on the ground.

Wow!

At first getting my balance standing up was hard enough. And I was still holding on to the sofa. Even so with two feet on the ground and one hand holding on I still did a lot of wobbling and falling.

One of the things that I noticed was that with every day I was getting less wobbly while standing up. That also meant that I did less falling and more standing and I even did a semi-walk, always holding on to the sofa. I was beginning to think I might soon be able to take a step, or two, but not three without holding on. I thought about it every time that I stood up. But it was really quite scary, even though I knew I was going to have to do it. So, when I was ready to go for it I decided to wait for mum and dad both to be in the room. It seemed daft to do my first walk with no one to watch.

Then I started. First I stood up holding on to the sofa. Then, I looked up to make sure mum and dad were paying attention. I was really concentrating. I knew I had to let go of the sofa and then take those steps. Off I went one step, then two, wobble, wobble and almost a third step but no that was it. I could tell by the big smiles on mum and dad faces that they thought it was great. It was great. I had taken my first steps. I could walk – well, at least I had taken my first wobbly steps. It really was great to be up and moving.

Chapter 11 Talk To Me

I've told you already about the strange language some adults use when they talk to me. Really my aunt used to do it all the time.

'Doh, doh, doh,' she uttered. Then, 'Ga, ga, ga.'

That's when I made a big mistake. 'Ga, ga, ga,' was quite easy. So instead of ignoring the silly talk from my aunt like I usually did, I replied.

'Ga, ga, ga.'

Big mistake.

'He can talk,' screeched my aunt. 'Listen he can talk, ga, ga, ga.'

I'm not replying, I thought. No way am I going to use such ridiculous words, or non-words, again. So instead I just smiled up at my aunt.

'Ga, ga, ga,' she tried again. And by this time there were a lot of adult faces looking down at me. I just smiled again. I'm not going to make that mistake twice. I decided I would wait until I could really talk before I followed an adult who spoke to me.

When I was very young the talk time that I liked best was when my dad dried me after a lovely bath. He would always lift me out of the bath and wrap me in a big towel that was all soft and fluffy. Then he would sit down and put me on his thighs where I could look up at him. Then he went all round my face pointing to different parts. It didn't take me long to work out he was giving me the names.

'Nose,' he said with his finger on that bump in the middle of my face.

I didn't try straight away to repeat what he said. It's too difficult I thought. Instead I gave my dad a big smile so that he would know I really liked this game.

'Mouth,' he said pointing to where the milk went in. I gave him a really big smile for that word because I knew I would soon be having my last bottle of milk for the day.

'Eye,' he said. Be careful I thought I don't like things coming too close to the bit that helps me to see.

'Ears, chin.'

I'll have to learn all of those I thought.

'Teeth – oh dear it's gums really for you,' said dad.

'These are my teeth,' continued dad as he tapped on those white things that are so sore coming through.

'Hair, your hair's growing, isn't it?'

I like dad going through all those names with me. It was hard at first to remember each one. But now I think can remember them all. I'll say them to dad when I'm a little bit older.

The strangest lot of talk comes when mum takes me out in the buggy. As soon as we leave the house mum starts to talk. I didn't know, at first, that she was talking to me. But then I realised she was. She was talking to me and she talks to me all the time.

'Look at that, Christopher.'

'That's a big red bus.'

'Wow, it's really big isn't it?'

When mum says 'isn't it' I don't think she's waiting for me to reply, because she hardly pauses before carrying on talking.

'Look at the green leaves on the tree.'

'Can you see them?'

'They're moving around today, aren't they?'

'That's the wind doing that.'

'Whoosh, goes the wind.'

I never know what mum's going to talk about. She seems ready to talk about anything.

'Look at that big lorry.'

'It's almost as big as the bus, isn't it?'

'But it's not red, is it?'

'It's a blue one.'

Colours are a bit tricky because there are so many of them. Yellow, white, black, purple, pink, orange, there are just so many of them.

Sometimes, mum even stops to talk about something.

'Did you see that lorry?'

'It's delivering things to the shops, isn't it?'

I just smile. I'll talk to her about it all when I'm bigger. Mind you, at first it was a bit embarrassing because she talked in a loud voice so lots of people could hear her, not just me. But then I started to like it, and now I really enjoy the walks and mum talking to me. We go out almost every day and I really look forward to doing that.

The other good time for talk was when we were having some food and we all sat around the table. Well, I sat in my high chair and had straps on to keep me from getting out. Mind you, I didn't want to try to get out. I liked having some food and anyway what would I do if I got out? It was too far to the floor.

'Is that nice, Christopher?'

It was a bit like being out in the pusher. Mum, or dad, would ask a question but they didn't wait for an answer before going on to something else.

Then I noticed as I got older that most people used real talk. So no more,

'Ga, ga, ga.'

I was pleased with that because it was good to hear lots and lots of words and sentences. It really helped me to learn new words and understand what was being said. I was beginning to think I might start to talk very soon. Well, I might try one word at a time to start with. Two words and longer sentences might have to wait for a little while.

Chapter 12 Lots And Lots Of Books

I love books. They're great. And there are so many of them.
I've got some on a low shelf in my bedroom at home. Then,
wow. I couldn't believe how many there were at the
Library. They have special shelves for books there and some
boxes with big books for children like me. I love books.

It all started soon after I was born. Dad was sitting down
and he got me and held me in his arms and started to read a
book with me. I couldn't believe it. All those coloured
pictures of different animals, toys and things which I knew
we had at home. Although I said dad read a book with me
that wasn't really what happened at the start. At first dad
sort of talked me through each page.

'Look at that animal, Christopher.'

'He's big isn't he?'

'Look at that long snake. Can you see it?'

Although dad kept asking me questions I don't think he expected me to answer. So I didn't. I just enjoyed looking at all the different pictures and listening to dad telling me all about it. I like hearing lots of new things about the pictures.

Of course, sometimes mum or dad would just plain read to me and that's good too. I like the big Nursery Rhymes book that we've got at home. I enjoy the rhymes, even though sometimes it sounds a bit weird to me.

'The dish ran away with the spoon.'

How strange is that? We've dishes and spoons in our house but they don't seem to do any running. And before that there was,

'Hey diddle, diddle, the cat and the fiddle.'

I've seen quite a few cats near my house. I've seen black ones and black and white cats. I've even seen a ginger cat. But I've never seen one with fiddle.

Then there's Humpty Dumpty. He sat on a wall. But every time we have that rhyme he falls off the wall. You would think after all this time he would have learned to sit still and not fall. But no, he keeps on doing it. I think some of the nursery rhymes must just be pretend stories.

The thing with books is that I like my mum and dad to read a story to me again, again and again. That way I really get to know them well. And once I could crawl and sit up I could look at a hardback book all by myself. So I could remind myself of the story. At first it was tricky but then I learned to get the book the right way up and turn the pages all by myself.

I think when I really get started with my talking I'll be able to look at a book and remember the whole story in my head. Then I might even join in the reading and say a few of the words, especially the rhyming ones. I think mum and dad will like me joining in like that.

I like the books about different railway engines. Thomas, the blue one, does lots of different things on his journeys. They're great. And there are lots of other Thomas railway books about other engines and carriages that go on different journeys as well. I've even been to the railway station near my house a few times and seen lots of different trains coming in or going out of the station. None of them look like Thomas but it doesn't matter. I could sit and watch them all day if I was given the chance. We even went on a train once. My dad took me. We only went one station and then we changed platforms and came back. But that was great; I like the trains.

I've even got some books with a great big bear in them. And it's coloured purple. He does lots of different things in the stories. I like all my animal books; I've got some with a gang of big and small dogs; although the black and white tom cat seems to be able to scare them. And there are books about a dog that has got a spot. Some of those books are funny. Then there are the dinosaurs, I'm not quite sure about them. They seem to be very, very big. There are some with long necks, others with spikes on their backs, and some that even manage to fly. And some of them look as though they could be really fierce, especially that one that my dad calls T-Rex. It's got really big teeth! Then there is the story of the boy with a favourite book. I really like that book. But I can't decide yet which is my favourite book.

So I've got some great books where my dad and I look at the pictures and dad tells me the story. But can you believe it, my dad, when he's on his own, even reads books without any pictures in it. That must be really tricky. I haven't worked out yet what he does. When my dad is reading I've even heard him say to my mum;

'Listen to what it says here.'

And then he usually reads from the book, just like when he reads to me, except there aren't any pictures to help with the reading. So how clever is that then?

I'm curious to find out how he does it. I think it might be something to do with those black circles and lines and squiggles on the page. I'll try and work that out later. I've even tried making some of those shapes when I use my big crayon on a sheet of paper. But I just get a lot of lines all over the place. Still it doesn't matter for the moment as long as mum and dad keep reading to me. I can look at all the

pictures and hear the great stories. I love books.

Chapter 13 Birthday Cake

There are so many exciting things that happen every day. And there are lots of different foods that I'm looking forward to trying. A few days ago my mum made some cup-cakes. Well, that's what she called them. But they don't really look like one of the cups that I drink from.

Anyway my mum said, 'would you like some cupcake?' So it didn't sound as though I was going to get a whole one. I just smiled, because that would tell my mum I'd like to try some. And it was lovely. I had some pink sticky stuff on top of my bit of cup-cake and that was so sweet. Yummy. So that's another food that I really like. So what with chocolate biscuits and ice cream I could tell that eating yummy food was going to be really good. Mind you, even now I've always got lots of different fruits to eat. They are yummy too and sweet but in a different way to the sticky cakes.

Then one day there seemed to be a lot of whispering going on in the kitchen. Just as I was trying to work out what was going on mum and dad came out of the kitchen and started to sing to me.

'Happy birthday to you,

Happy birthday to you,

Happy birthday dear Christopher,

Happy birthday to you.'

Then they clapped and smiled and laughed, and dad had carried in a large plate with a cake on it. The cake even looked like Thomas, the blue railway engine. It was a lot bigger than the cup-cakes. And it looked like it had some of that sticky sweet stuff all over it. On top of that was a candle with a flickering flame at the top.

They kept saying, 'Blow out the candle, Christopher.'

That was really not very easy. They kept showing me what to do, but I couldn't manage it, even though I tried to do a big puff. So, in the end dad and I had to do it together. And then we did manage to blow out the flame. So the blowing was really hard, but I did like the piece of cake they gave me to eat. I had only had that small piece of cup-cake to eat before, especially with so much sweet icing on it. Now I had a bigger piece of cake and with icing on top and all around the sides as well. And this time the icing was in different colours, yummy.

In fact it was so yummy that I said,

'Ta.'

Really I wanted to say thank you, but it didn't come out of my mouth sounding like thank you. Not that it mattered. Mum and dad just loved me saying, 'Ta.'

'Who's a big boy, saying thank you,' said dad. There's another one of those big boys again. I think I'll keep on getting those for ages.

As they seemed to like me talking so much I did it again for them.

'Ta.'

And each time I said 'Ta' they really liked it. So what with a special cake and a candle on top it was a great day. And I think the 'Happy Birthday' part means that I really am one year old now. And my name is Christopher.